FRANCIS SCOTT KEY

O say can you see ~~through~~ by the dawn's early light,
What so proudly we hail'd at the twilight's last gleaming,
Whose broad stripes & bright stars through the perilous fight
O'er the ramparts we watch'd were so gallantly streaming?
And the rocket's red glare, the bomb bursting in air
Gave proof through the night that our flag was still there,
O say does that star spangled banner yet wave
O'er the land of the free & the home of the brave?

On the shore dimly seen through the mists of the deep,
Where the foe's haughty host in dread silence reposes,
What is that which the breeze, o'er the towering steep,
As it fitfully blows, half conceals, half discloses?
Now it catches the gleam of the morning's first beam,
In full glory reflected now shines in the stream,
'Tis the star-spangled banner — O long may it wave
O'er the land of the free & the home of the brave!

And where is that band who so vauntingly swore,
That the havoc of war & the battle's confusion
A home & a Country should leave us no more?
~~Their blood~~
— Their blood has wash'd out their foul footstep's pollution
No refuge could save the hireling & slave
From the terror of flight or the gloom of the grave,
And the star-spangled banner in triumph doth wave
O'er the land of the free & the home of the brave.

O thus be it ever when freemen shall stand
Between their lov'd home & the war's desolation!
Blest with vict'ry & peace may the heav'n rescued land
Praise the power that hath made & preserv'd us a nation.
Then conquer we must, when our cause it is just,
And this be our motto — "In God is our trust"
And the star-spangled banner in triumph shall wave
O'er the land of the free & the home of the brave. —

FRANCIS SCOTT KEY

Melissa Whitcraft

A FIRST BOOK

FRANKLIN WATTS
New York / Chicago / London / Toronto / Sydney

Cover illustration by Lisa Steinberg

Photographs copyright ©: Maryland Historical Society, Baltimore, Md.:
pp. 2, 17, 25, 26, 34, 44; Reuters/Bettmann: p. 10; North Wind Picture
Archives, Alfred, Me.: pp. 14, 15, 18, 23, 27, 30, 31, 39, 41, 45, 48, 52;
Maryland State Archives: p. 20 (#MSA SC 907); Anne S. K. Brown Military
Collection, Brown University Library: p. 32; The Peale Museum, Baltimore
City Life Museums: p. 36; Jay Mallin: pp. 43, 54, 59; Stock Montage,
Chicago: p. 51; Archive Photos/Carlin: p.57.

Library of Congress Cataloging-in-Publication Data

    Francis Scott Key / by Melissa Whitcraft.
        p. cm. — (First book)
    Includes bibliographical references and index.
    ISBN 0-531-20163-5
    1. Key, Francis Scott, 1779–1843—Biography—Juvenile litera-
ture. 2. Poets, American—19th century—Biography—Juvenile literature.
3. United States—History—War of 1812—Biography—Juvenile literature.
[1. Key, Francis Scott, 1779–1843. 2. Poets, American. 3. Lawyers. 4. Star-
spangled banner (Song)] I. Title. II. Series.
PS2168.W48 1994
349.73'092 — dc20
[B]   94-2571
                                                CIP AC

CONTENTS

For
ECRW,
with love

FRANCIS SCOTT KEY

The "Dream Team" stands proudly as "The Star-Spangled Banner" is played after winning the gold medal in basketball at the 1992 summer Olympics in Barcelona, Spain.

INTRODUCTION

$\mathcal{E}$very time Americans go to a ball game or attend a national ceremony, they stand to sing "The Star-Spangled Banner." Their voices ring out with:

> *Oh, say can you see by the dawn's early light*
> *What so proudly we hail'd at the twilight's last gleaming,*
> *Whose broad stripes and bright stars through the perilous fight*
> *O'er the ramparts we watched were so gallantly streaming?*
> *And the rockets' red glare, the bombs bursting in air,*
> *Gave proof through the night that our flag was still there.*
> *Oh, say does that star-spangled banner yet wave*
> *O'er the land of the free and the home of the brave?*

The description of the battle in this song makes Americans proud of their flag and country. But, what of the man who wrote the words? Who was he?

His name was Francis Scott Key. He was born on August 1, 1779, three years after the first American patriots signed the Declaration of Independence from Great Britain.

On September 13, 1814, Francis Scott Key's life and his country's history came together at the Battle of Fort McHenry. The events Key witnessed at that time inspired him to write the poem whose first stanza appears above. That poem was destined to be set to music and become the national anthem of the United States.

Key's accomplishments, however, did not begin and end that dramatic night in Baltimore Harbor. He was more than a poet. He was also a thoughtful lawyer, a committed public servant, and a devoted family man. In these roles, Francis Scott Key, an ordinary citizen, committed his life to upholding the principles of freedom fought for in 1776.

1
EARLY LIFE AND EDUCATION

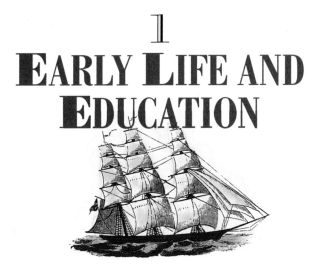

$\mathcal{F}$rancis Scott Key was born into a wealthy colonial family. In 1720, his great-grandfather Philip Key traded the known comforts of a well-connected life in England for the unfamiliar sights and sounds of the English colony of Maryland, where he became a successful lawyer.

Key's father, John Ross Key, fought in the American Revolution. He was also a judge and a farmer. At the time of his son's birth in 1779, he owned a 3,000-acre (1,200-ha) plantation in Frederick, Maryland, called Terra Rubra. The name of Francis's first home means "red land" and refers to the rich red clay found in the ground of the plantation.

The Key plantation was spectacular. Surrounded by rolling fields, shaded woods, quiet streams, and breathtaking views of the distant Blue Ridge Mountains, it was an idyllic place to grow up during America's first years of peaceful independence.

*This engraving of the young Francis Scott Key
was made from an oil painting.*

As was typical of many eighteenth-century plantations, Terra Rubra was run by slaves who grew the crops and provided most of the other necessities of life. Besides the impressive main house, which contained a separate wing for the slave quarters, the plantation had many surrounding outbuildings. There was a stone house for fruits and vegetables, a smokehouse for meats, and a special building for weaving, sewing, and candle making. There were also barns for the animals and a blacksmith shop.

The plantation was isolated, but Key was not lonely. He had a loving relationship with his parents and a lasting

Key would have used a road similar to this one traveling to and from Terra Rubra.

friendship with his younger sister, Anne. Family closeness was important because there were no near neighbors, and the Keys seldom went into town.

When friends and relations visited the large reception rooms of the main house were thrown open. Terra Rubra was known to be a friendly house, and all visitors were welcomed as important links to the world beyond.

Because there were no schools near the plantation, Key and his sister were educated at first by their parents. Their father taught them the history of the Revolution and described all he saw on his travels through the county as a judge. Their mother taught them to read and write and to appreciate the beauty of poetry.

Their mother also taught the slaves to read and write and conducted prayer services for them. Young Francis attended these services and learned early in life to respect all people.

Francis's paternal grandmother, Ann Arnold Key, was another great influence in Key's early life. She lived in a beautiful mansion near Annapolis, Maryland. She had lost her sight trying to rescue two slaves from a fire in her father's house, and young Key was her link to the written word. He spent hours reading books to her. It is said that his great ability as a public speaker grew out of these special hours he spent with his grandmother.

At age ten, Francis left Terra Rubra to attend school in Annapolis, and it may be that his grandmother persuaded him to go. In any event, he entered the recently opened St.

Francis Scott Key's beloved grandmother, Ann Arnold Ross Key,
and his paternal grandfather, Francis Key

 17

George Washington bade farewell to his officers in Annapolis, where a few years later the young Key attended school.

John's Grammar School there and lived with his grandmother's sister, who had a house near the campus.

When he arrived in the fall of 1789, Francis knew Annapolis was an important city in the history of the country. Congress had met in its State House, and George Washington had used this same State House to give his farewell speech when he resigned his commission in the Continental Army.

As exciting as the atmosphere in the town was, young Key was not happy. He wrote of this period, "Sad was the parting [from Terra Rubra], sad the days, and dull the school and dull the plays."

Eventually, Francis did adjust to St. John's. He took daily classes in grammar, studied poetry, and made friends. He also learned Latin and Greek. Educators of the time believed true education did not begin until students knew these ancient languages.

At fourteen, Francis enrolled in the freshman class at St. John's College. Over the next three years he studied such varied subjects as algebra, trigonometry, metaphysics, navigation, and geography. He also read the ancient Greek philosophers Plato and Aristotle.

A classmate described Francis as being slight of build but always willing "to throw himself into any plan for amusement." And yet Francis was also deeply religious. Many of his friends studied *The Age of Reason*, a controversial view of religion written by Thomas Paine. Francis didn't. He would not read an author who criticized the traditional interpretation of the Bible.

St. John's campus in Annapolis, Maryland

Francis was graduated from St. John's with honors when he was seventeen. He was the class valedictorian. He would later become a loyal and lifelong supporter of the school he had once thought "dull."

The choices Key made as an adult reflected all of his early experiences. He would spend his life commited to his family and his country. In addition, his religious faith, his concern for the slaves, and his love of poetry would never leave him.

2
STARTING OUT

After seven years of study at St. John's, Francis Scott Key was ready to choose a profession. As much as he loved Terra Rubra, he did not return to run it. His education had prepared him for a far different life.

The deeply religious Key was interested in the ministry. However, at the suggestion of his uncle, who was a lawyer, Key chose the law. This decision would have far-reaching ramifications during the War of 1812. For now, it meant Key studied law with a prominent judge and lived with his uncle in Annapolis.

This same uncle introduced Key to Mary Tayloe Lloyd. Mary, or Polly as Key called her, interested the young law student greatly. He wrote her poems and said about her, "Perhaps she'll value more my love, Perhaps give more of hers to me, Perhaps may greet me with a smile more

*Washington, D.C., in 1810 —
the new National City,
full of promise and dusty roads*

sweet, if smile more sweet can be." Polly did greet Key "with a smile more sweet," and in 1802 they were married.

At first Key practiced law in Frederick, Maryland, but when he joined his uncle's law firm in Washington, D.C., he and Mary settled in nearby Georgetown, Maryland, a thriving tobacco port. A lovely town, it was a far nicer place to raise a family than the new National City, which was little more than a dusty village with muddy roads when it rained.

Key took over his uncle's practice in 1806. Soon he had his first chance to argue a case in front of the United States Supreme Court.

It was 1807. Thomas Jefferson was president. Aaron Burr, who had been vice president during Jefferson's first term, was accused of treason. There was some evidence that he was attempting to set up a new country west of the Mississippi River.

When this plot was uncovered, two of Burr's messengers, Justus Erich Bollman and Samuel Swartwout, were arrested and brought from New Orleans to Washington, D.C., to be tried as traitors.

Key argued that the Constitution defined treason as an overt act that existed only when a citizen waged war or helped others wage war directly against the United States. Because Bollman and Swartwout had not tried to overthrow the government with direct force, Key said, they had not committed treason.

In his elegant defense, Key also argued that Bollman and Swartwout could not even be tried because they had

The Georgetown mansion where Key and Polly raised their large family

President Thomas Jefferson was not pleased when Key won his first case in front of the Supreme Court.

been illegally arrested. The two men had been taken into custody and imprisoned in Washington, D.C., without due process of the law.

There were many in Jefferson's administration, including the president himself, who wanted to see Bollman and Swartwout convicted. Key's arguments, however, were so strong and the evidence against the two men so weak that the Supreme Court had to acquit them.

The Bollman-Swartwout trial caused quite a sensation and established Key's career. Those who heard his defense were greatly impressed with the twenty-eight-year-old lawyer.

Aaron Burr rallying supporters to his cause around the time Bollman and Swartwout were arrested in New Orleans, Louisiana.

As important as the case was to Key's growing practice, it was also an excellent example of how the judiciary branch of the government (the Supreme Court) can and should act independently from the wishes of the executive branch (the president). Jefferson may not have been happy with the verdict, but it proved that the checks and balances in government worked.

Key also showed a commitment to his community that was a natural extension of his commitment to the law. His reputation as a brilliant, articulate lawyer spread, but he continued to represent people who could not afford his fees. In fact, he never even charged a fee to soldiers who had fought in the Revolutionary War.

If his concern for society made him a lawyer for all the people, his faith in God made him an active member of his church. Hymns he wrote can still be found in the Episcopal Church hymnal.

Perhaps because his own experience at St. John's had been so positive, Key understood the importance of giving all children a good education. At thirty, he joined the Lancaster Society, which ran a school in Georgetown specifically designed for children whose parents could not afford private school tuitions.

Key believed citizens had to reach beyond the comforts of their own lives to help others. Some of the positions he took were popular; others weren't. All demonstrated his conviction that everyone must be socially responsible.

3
"BOMBS BURSTING IN AIR"

Throughout Key's childhood and first years in Georgetown, the United States was at peace. There were rumblings, however, that eventually led the new country into another confrontation with Great Britain.

The British, at war with the French since 1803, refused to allow neutral nations, such as the United States, to trade with France unless they inspected the goods first. In retaliation, the French refused to accept any cargo that had been inspected by the British. These inspections and subsequent embargoes severely limited the United States' ability to get its goods to the European markets.

In addition, as the fighting with France took its toll on their navy, the British began to take sailors off American ships to fight on British warships. The Americans protested, but the British said they were only taking back their own sailors who had deserted.

Before the War of 1812, British naval officers routinely took American sailors to serve on their ships against their will.

Eventually the United States felt it had to act. On June 18, 1812, the government declared war on Great Britain. The War of 1812 had begun.

The early years of the war were not easy for the United States. Soldiers were not well trained, and many battles were lost. There were also those who questioned the wisdom of fighting against the British again. The New England merchants felt that if it had been difficult before, now it would be impossible to trade on the world market.

Key had ambivalent feelings about the war, but when the British fleet entered Chesapeake Bay on August 19,

British ships blockaded Chesapeake Bay in preparation for the battle of Fort McHenry.

*Washington, D.C.,
ablaze in the War of 1812*

1814, he became a volunteer aide in the local militia. The war was in his own backyard, and he wanted to help.

The Americans, however, were no match for the professional English troops. On August 24, the British captured Washington, D.C., and burned down many of its new government buildings.

Immediately after this attack the British army headed back to its ships in Chesapeake Bay. On the way, three disorderly British soldiers were arrested by a civilian American doctor named William Beanes. The British then arrested Dr. Beanes for interfering with their military and took him to their flagship, the H.M.S. *Tonnant*.

Dr. Beanes was an old family friend of Key's. When Key heard what had happened, he appealed to President James Madison, who sent him to John Skinner, the U.S. agent in charge of prisoner exchanges. Together they set out for the English fleet. Key hoped his abilities as a lawyer would convince the British to let Dr. Beanes go.

Eventually the British did agree to release him, but they did not allow any of the Americans to return to shore. The British were planning to attack Baltimore and to prevent the Americans from warning anyone they removed Key and the others from the flagship and made them wait out the battle on a smaller boat. They were out of danger there, but in full view of what was to come.

To capture Baltimore, the British knew they first had to take Fort McHenry, which guarded the ocean approach to the city. Carefully, they maneuvered sixteen of their smaller

The "bombs bursting in air"
during the terrifying
battle at Fort McHenry

ships up the Patapsco River and placed them in two half circles around the fort. On September 13, the ships began their bombardment.

The fort fired back, but the cannon shots fell short. Anchored 2 miles (3.2 km) offshore, the British ships were out of range of the fort's inferior cannons. There was nothing the American defenders could do but wait for the shelling to stop.

The British bombarded the fort all day and night. Windows in Baltimore shook. The air in the harbor was heavy with the smell of gunpowder. It was a terrible battle. Key witnessed it all: the huge "bombs bursting in air" and the bright "rockets' red glare."

During the night the British landed troops to storm the fort from the rear. Key and the others heard the assault and listened to the eerie silence that followed. When dawn finally broke, they did not know if the attack had succeeded.

Key looked over at Fort McHenry. Because there was no wind, he could not tell whose flag was flying. Then, a slight breeze unfurled the flag at the fort. It was the Stars and Stripes! Eighteen hundred shells had been fired at the fort during a twenty-five-hour period, but miraculously the Americans had withstood both the shelling and the assault by British troops.

Key was overjoyed. Quickly he wrote down the beginnings of a poem.

That day the British withdrew their remaining troops and sailed for open ocean. Without Fort McHenry, they could not take Baltimore. Without Baltimore, they could not establish a stronghold on American soil.

Key learning that the battle of Fort McHenry had been won, in a painting by Edward Percy Moran

Key and his friends returned to Baltimore. That night he finished his poem and showed it to his brother-in-law, telling him he thought it should be set to a popular tune known as "To Anacreon in Heaven." Key's brother-in-law took the poem to a printer. Initially the verses were published under the title "The Defense of Fort McHenry," and the author was listed simply as "a gentleman of Maryland."

By October, newspapers around the country were printing the poem. It was also being sung in theaters and had been renamed "The Star-Spangled Banner." Key's song became a unifying cry to help the Americans fight the war.

On December 24, 1814, the United States and Great Britain signed a peace treaty. The reasons the United States had gone to war in the first place, the seizure of its ships and sailors, weren't even mentioned in the settlement.

The battle for Baltimore might have been relegated to a military footnote in history if Key's words hadn't immortalized the courage of the soldiers at Fort McHenry.

4
THE QUESTION OF SLAVERY

*K*ey knew slavery was morally wrong. He once wrote, "Where else, except in slavery, was ever such a bed of torture prepared by man for man?"

As eloquent as these words were, however, Key did not feel the "bed of torture" could be dismantled overnight. For him, immediate emancipation was impossible because slavery was such an integral part of the American economy.

Key had been raised on a slave-run plantation. He knew how important slave labor was for the plantation owners. To save plantations from financial ruin, Key believed, slavery had to end "gradually." He felt the owners needed time to "substitute other labor" for the slave workers they would lose with emancipation.

Key also thought the slaves themselves, many of whom had spent their lives on one farm, needed time to prepare "for the change in their condition."

Enchained slaves being marched through Washington, D.C., as Key would have seen them

Key's position on slavery was also influened by his strong commitment to the law. As a lawyer he often defended slaves. A contemporary said of him, "He was their [the slaves'] advocate in courts of justice, pressing their rights to the extent of the law and ready to brave . . . even personal danger in their behalf."

Even though he was an advocate for slaves, Key would not defend anyone who took part in slave rebellions. To him these protests were illegal.

In 1836, as district attorney for the District of Columbia, he prosecuted the abolitionist Dr. Crandall for inciting slaves to riot. As the government's prosecutor, Key said Crandall had broken the law because a slaveholding community's right to protection was more important than the "right of others to excite . . . insurrection."

It was clear when he prosecuted Crandall that Key believed the law came before freedom obtained by breaking the law. Nevertheless, he often used the law to try to free slaves.

In 1825, eleven years before the Crandall case, a Spanish slave trader, the *Antelope*, was captured by American privateers, who put the slaves on their ship. This ship was then captured by an American government ship, which brought the slaves into the United States.

The Spanish demanded their slaves be returned because the United States and Spain had signed a treaty stating that any property discovered in the hands of pirates had to be returned to its rightful owner.

In a "touching and persuasive" defense of the captured slaves, the forty-five-year-old Key argued this case before the

Supreme Court. He said that the slaves were not Spanish property because they were human beings and "by Law of Nature . . . free." He further argued that because the case was being tried in the United States, United States law had to be enforced. He then pointed out that at this time the country's law not only prohibited slave trade, but also, through the Slave Trade Acts, demanded that slaves brought into the country be set free.

Chief Justice Marshall sided with Spain, however, saying, "This court must not yield to feelings which might

John Marshall, the chief justice who rejected Key's arguments in the Antelope *case*

seduce it from the path of duty, but must obey the mandate of the law." The international treaty concerning property rights proved more powerful than Key's heartfelt plea for the law of nature.

Key must have been disappointed that he lost the case. He wanted slaves to be freed, but he knew that once free they would face many problems. In early nineteenth-century America, free blacks had their freedom, but little else. It was hard for them to get work. They were treated as outcasts and not welcomed in white communities. It is difficult to understand today, but the American Colonization Society, an organization founded in 1817, thought the best way to address these injustices was to offer the freed slaves a new life in Africa, the "land of their fathers." The Society acted on this belief by establishing a colony for freed slaves on the west coast of Africa. Begun with President Monroe's approval, this colony was named Liberia, from the Latin word *liber*, meaning "free." Liberia exists today as an independent nation approximately the size of Ohio.

Like President Monroe, Key supported the American Colonization Society. However, many antislavery groups criticized the Society's colonization plan. They felt freed slaves should be brought into American society, not shipped out to a land many had never seen. They also believed it wrong to colonize freed blacks as a way to keep them from influencing their enslaved brothers to fight for freedom. Finally, they ridiculed the Society as a group of "idealists with troubled consciences" men and women who didn't believe in slavery but who owned slaves themselves.

INFORMATION

ABOUT GOING TO LIBERIA.

THINGS WHICH EVERY EMIGRANT TO LIBERIA OUGHT TO KNOW.

COMMON OBJECTIONS

TO GOING TO LIBERIA ANSWERED,

REPLY

TO CERTAIN CAVILINGS AGAINST COLONIZATION.

&c., &c.

The title page from a book published by the
American Colonization Society explaining
their emigration policy

Maryland in Liberia, *by John B. Latrobe, shows what the new black emigrants found when they first arrived in Africa.*

Key was an antislavery idealist who owned slaves, and his attitude toward slavery was confusing. He freed many slaves during his lifetime, but left others to his wife in his will. Apparently, he hoped she would free them before she died.

He hated slavery, but because he supported the American Colonization Society, he was criticized by abolitionists, by southerners who thought he was an abolitionist, and by freed blacks who thought he wanted to force all of them back to Africa.

After the Civil War a freed black man chooses his own road.

Yet, despite all the criticism, Key continued to work for the Society. As he explained once in an address to Congress, "If colonization resulted in the complete abolition of slavery . . . who can doubt that of all the blessings we may be permitted to bequeath to our descendents, this will receive the richest tribute of their thanks and veneration?"

Key's attempt to solve the social and moral dilemma of slavery through gradual and legal means was destined to fail. It would take the bloody battles of the Civil War to provide a final answer to the painful question of slavery in the United States.

5
A GENTLEMAN OF MARYLAND

$\mathcal{G}$iven Key's conservative stand on slavery, it is not surprising that contemporaries described him as "a staid and sober minded man" who disapproved of theater and "vain amusements." Key was deeply committed to family, church, and country. There was little time in his life for frivolity.

Yet, it would be unfair to describe Key as cold and unimaginative. For one thing, as much as he disapproved of "vain amusements," he was known to enjoy his pipe and parties where he smoked, drank whiskey, and charmed friends with amusing, spontaneously written verse. He was even capable of writing silly poems to entertain his eleven children. One of those poems was written on an egg: "Look for the hen with yellow legs, For she's the hen that lays these eggs."

Like this gentleman of "Old Maryland,"
Key also enjoyed his pipe.

A clue to Key's personality can be found also in his more serious poetry and his other writings. His passionate feelings for the United States cry out in the rousing words of the "Star-Spangled Banner." His heartfelt arguments against slavery show us that he really did see slavery as an evil "bed of torture."

Other poems were tender expressions of thoughts closest to his heart. He remembered his childhood at Terra Rubra in this poem to his sister:

I think of thee—of those bright hours,
Rich in life's first and fairest flow'rs,
When childhood's gay delights were ours,

My sister!

The mountain top—the wood, the plain,
The winding creek—the shaded lane
Shall shine in both our eyes again,

My sister!

In a hymn he wrote in 1819, Key said, "Since words can never measure, let my life show forth thy praise." As an older man, Key continued to believe that what he did would "measure" the value of his life more than what he said. Another man might have retired to spend his remaining years with his large family at his beloved plantation, but Key never retired from his sense of duty.

After almost thirty years in Georgetown, he moved with Polly and four of their children to Washington, D.C. There Key continued to practice law and argue important cases in front of the Supreme Court.

In 1833, President Andrew Jackson, who was an old friend of Key's, sent the well-known lawyer to Alabama to intervene between angry settlers and federal officials. The settlers had built their homes on land promised to the Creek Indians and were asked to resettle. Three thousand refused. When soldiers tried to force them to leave the land, riots broke out and people were killed.

President Jackson was afraid these hostilities would lead to civil war. He sent Key to resolve the dispute because he believed this elegant and diplomatic emissary would be able to negotiate a peaceful settlement.

When Key first arrived, the local officials were suspicious. They saw him as Jackson's spokesman and assumed he would be indifferent to their cause. However, Key was also the man who wrote the "Star-Spangled Banner," so they gave him a chance.

Using his strong legal abilities and endearing personal charm, Key was able to calm the fears of the settlers and negotiate a compromise everyone could live with. As one biographer described Key, he was a "tolerant Marylander" who knew how to handle delicate situations.

The same year that President Jackson sent Key to Alabama, he made his friend the district attorney for Washington, D.C. One case Key prosecuted during this time was the trial of Dr. Crandall.

*Washington, D.C., in 1837, when
Key was appointed to his second term
as district attorney*

President Andrew Jackson, who respected Key despite their differences, greeting supporters on his way to Washington after his election

Another trial involved the prosecution of a man named Richard Lawrence. Lawrence was accused of trying to assassinate President Jackson for political reasons. The president wanted Lawrence to be given the stiffest punishment possible. Key recommended that Lawrence be put in an asylum. He was convinced the man was insane.

President Jackson was furious that his district attorney went against his wishes. Many others also criticized Key's compassionate position. As he had in the Bollman-Swartwout case, however, Key followed his own conscience rather than give in to the wishes of his friends.

Despite their disagreement, Key remained Jackson's district attorney. In fact, before Jackson turned the presidency over to Martin Van Buren, he nominated Key for a second term. The Senate confirmed this appointment in January 1837. Key was to remain district attorney until 1841.

Key may never have retired, but he also never abandoned his deep feeling for Terra Rubra. Whenever possible, he returned to his boyhood home. With his children and grandchildren, he continued to explore the creeks and woods he had so happily discovered with his sister.

One of the last times Key was at Terra Rubra, in 1842 after a trip out West with his son, he wrote, "There has not been for twenty years such a harvest. The valley seems to laugh and sing."

Key would not see another harvest. In the winter of 1842 he caught a bad cold. A poem he wrote at the time

The Francis Scott Key Memorial in
Mount Olivet Cemetery, Frederick, Maryland

contained the line, "and sorrow, and sickness and death will come."

Death did come. On January 11, 1843, Francis Scott Key, husband, father, lawyer, and poet died. He had been a friend to presidents and a crusader for ordinary citizens. He had owned slaves, but tried to end slavery. His imprint on American law can be found in all the cases he argued before the Supreme Court.

Yet, for all his influence, it is the power of his words written on September 14, 1814, that we remember best. By the 1850s "The Star-Spangled Banner" was found in schoolbooks. In 1916, President Woodrow Wilson made it the official song of the Armed Forces. Finally, on March 3, 1931, an act of Congress made "The Star-Spangled Banner" the national anthem of the United States.

Today at Fort McHenry, Key's birthplace, and his gravesite, the American flag flies twenty-four hours a day to honor the man who, through the passion of his words, gave his country one of its greatest expressions of patriotism.

THE STAR-SPANGLED BANNER

by Francis Scott Key

Oh, say can you see by the dawn's early light
What so proudly we hail'd at the twilight's last gleaming,
Whose broad stripes and bright stars through the perilous fight
O'er the ramparts we watch'd were so gallantly streaming?
And the rockets' red glare, the bombs bursting in air,
Gave proof through the night that our flag was still there.
Oh, say does that star-spangled banner yet wave
O'er the land of the free and the home of the brave?

On the shore dimly seen through the mists of the deep,
Where the foe's haughty host in dread silence reposes,
What is that which the breeze, o'er the towering steep,
As it fitfully blows, half conceals, half discloses?
Now it catches the gleam of the morning's first beam,
In full glory reflected now shines in the stream.
'Tis the star-spangled banner, oh long may it wave,
O'er the land of the free and the home of the brave!

And where is that band who so vauntingly swore
That the havoc of war and the battle's confusion
A home and a country should leave us no more?
Their blood had wash'd out their foul footstep's pollution.
No refuge could save the hireling and slave
From the terror of flight or the gloom of the grave,
And the star-spangled banner in triumph doth wave
O'er the land of the free and the home of the brave.

Oh, thus be it ever when freemen shall stand
Between their lov'd home and the war's desolation!
Blest with vict'ry and peace may the heav'n-rescued land
Praise the power that hath made and preserv'd us a nation!
Then conquer we must, when our cause it is just,
And this be our motto, "In God is our Trust,"
And the star-spangled banner in triumph shall wave
O'er the land of the free and the home of the brave.

The Fort McHenry flag that inspired "The Star-Spangled Banner" is now at the Smithsonian Museum of American History in Washington, D.C

FOR FURTHER READING

Kroll, Steven. *By the Dawn's Early Light: The Story of the Star Spangled Banner.* New York: Scholastic, 1993.

Lowitz, Sadyebeth. *Francis Scott Key.* Minneapolis: Lerner Publishing Company, 1967.

Mandrell, Louise. *Sunrise Over the Harbor.* Fort Worth, Tex.: Summit Group, 1993.

Patterson, Lillie. *Francis Scott Key: Poet and Patriot.* New York: Chelsea Juniors, 1991.

INDEX

ABOUT THE AUTHOR

*M*elissa Whitcraft lives in Montclair, New Jersey, with her husband, their two sons, and their dog. She has had a lifelong fascination with American history, received a Master's in Art in Theatre, and has written plays, poetry, and short stories. She has also published *Tales From One Street Over* and has just completed *Letters From One Street Over*, two chapter books for early elementary grade readers.